Activities *for the* Differentiated Classroom

Gayle H. Gregory • Carolyn Chapman

CORWIN PRESS
Classroom

For information:

CORWIN PRESS

Corwin Press
A SAGE Publications Company
2455 Teller Road
Thousand Oaks, California 91320
CorwinPress.com

SAGE, Ltd.
1 Oliver's Yard
55 City Road
London EC1Y 1SP
United Kingdom

SAGE India Pvt. Ltd.
B 1/I 1 Mohan Cooperative
Industrial Area
Mathura Road, New Delhi
India 110 044

SAGE Asia-Pacific Pvt. Ltd.
33 Pekin Street #02-01
Far East Square
Singapore 048763

Printed in the United States of America.

ISBN 978-1-4129-5338-2

This book is printed on acid-free paper.

07 08 09 10 11 10 9 8 7 6 5 4 3 2 1

Executive Editor: Kathleen Hex
Managing Developmental Editor: Christine Hood
Editorial Assistant: Anne O'Dell
Developmental Writer: Barbara Allman
Developmental Editor: Carolea Williams
Proofreader: Bette Darwin
Art Director: Anthony D. Paular
Cover Designer: Monique Hahn
Interior Production Artist: Karine Hovsepian

Activities *for the* Differentiated Classroom

GRADE **2**

TABLE OF CONTENTS

Connections to Standards

This chart shows the national academic standards that are covered in each chapter.

MATHEMATICS	Standards are covered on pages
Numbers and Operations—Understand numbers, ways of representing numbers, relationships among numbers, and number systems.	12
Algebra—Understand patterns, relations, and functions.	14
Geometry—Use visualization, spatial reasoning, and geometric modeling to solve problems.	17
Measurement—Understand measurable attributes of objects and the units, systems, and processes of measurement.	9, 10, 22
Data Analysis and Probability—Formulate questions that can be addressed with data, and collect, organize, and display relevant data to answer them.	19
Problem Solving—Solve problems that arise in mathematics and in other contexts.	24
Communication—Organize and consolidate mathematical thinking through communication.	26

SCIENCE	Standards are covered on pages
Physical Science—Understand properties of objects and materials.	38, 40
Life Science—Understand characteristics of organisms.	36
Life Science—Understand life cycles of organisms.	33
Life Science—Understand organisms and environments.	31, 42
Earth and Space Science—Understand changes in the earth and sky.	28
Science in Personal and Social Perspectives—Identify types of resources.	44

SOCIAL STUDIES	Standards are covered on pages
Understand culture and cultural diversity.	63
Understand the ways human beings view themselves in and over time.	47
Understand the interactions among people, places, and environments.	61
Understand interactions among individuals, groups, and institutions.	57
Understand how people create and change structures of power, authority, and governance.	53
Understand how people organize for the production, distribution, and consumption of goods and services.	65

Understand relationships among science, technology, and society.	55
Understand the ideals, principles, and practices of citizenship in a democratic republic.	49

LANGUAGE ARTS	Standards are covered on pages
Read a wide range of literature from many periods in many genres to build an understanding of the many dimensions (e.g., philosophical, ethical, aesthetic) of human experience.	72, 78
Apply a wide range of strategies to comprehend, interpret, evaluate, and appreciate texts. Draw on prior experience, interactions with other readers and writers, knowledge of word meaning and of other texts, word identification strategies, and understanding of textual features (e.g., sound-letter correspondence, sentence structure, context, graphics).	67, 77
Employ a wide range of strategies while writing, and use different writing process elements appropriately to communicate with different audiences for a variety of purposes.	80
Apply knowledge of language structure, language conventions (e.g., spelling and punctuation), media techniques, figurative language, and genre to create, critique, and discuss print and nonprint texts.	75
Participate as knowledgeable, reflective, creative, and critical members of a variety of literacy communities.	70

Introduction

As a teacher who has adopted the differentiated philosophy, you design instruction to embrace the diversity of the unique students in your classroom and strategically select tools to build a classroom where all students can succeed. This requires careful planning and a very large toolkit! You must make decisions about what strategies and activities best meet the needs of the students in your classroom at that time. It is not a "one size fits all" approach.

When planning for differentiated instruction, include the steps described below. Refer to the planning model in *Differentiated Instructional Strategies: One Size Doesn't Fit All, Second Edition* (Gregory & Chapman, 2007) for more detailed information.

1. Establish standards, essential questions, and expectations for the lesson or unit.

2. Identify content, including facts, vocabulary, and essential skills.

3. Activate prior knowledge. Preassess students' levels of readiness for the learning and collect data on students' interests and attitudes about the topic.

4. Determine what students need to learn and how they will learn it. Plan various activities that complement the learning styles and readiness levels of all students in this particular class. Locate appropriate resources or materials for all levels of readiness.

5. Apply the strategies and adjust to meet students' varied needs.

6. Decide how you will assess students' knowledge. Consider providing choices for students to demonstrate what they know.

Differentiation does not mean always tiering every lesson for three levels of complexity or challenge. It *does* mean finding interesting, engaging, and appropriate ways to help students learn new concepts and skills. The practical activities in this book are designed to support your differentiated lesson plans. They are not prepackaged units but rather activities you can incorporate into your plan for meeting the unique needs of the students in your classroom right now. Use these activities as they fit into differentiated lessons or units you are planning. They might be used for total group lessons, to reinforce learning with individuals or small groups, to focus attention, to provide additional rehearsal opportunities, or to assess knowledge. Your differentiated toolkit should be brimming with engaging learning opportunities. Take out those tools and start building success for all your students!

Put It Into Practice

Differentiation is a Philosophy

For years teachers planned "the lesson" and taught it to all students, knowing that some will get it and some will not. Faced with NCLB and armed with brain research, we now know that this method of lesson planning will not reach the needs of all students. Every student learns differently. In order to leave no child behind, we must teach differently.

Differentiation is a philosophy that enables teachers to plan strategically in order to reach the needs of the diverse learners in the classroom and to help them meet the standards. Supporters of differentiation as a philosophy believe:

- All students have areas of strength.

- All students have areas that need to be strengthened.

- Each student's brain is as unique as a fingerprint.

- It is never too late to learn.

- When beginning a new topic, students bring their prior knowledge base and experience to the new learning.

- Emotions, feelings, and attitudes affect learning.

- All students can learn.

- Students learn in different ways at different times.

The Differentiated Classroom

A differentiated classroom is one in which the teacher responds to the unique needs of the students in that room, at that time. Differentiated instruction provides a variety of options to successfully reach targeted standards. It meets learners where they are and offers challenging, appropriate options for them to achieve success.

Differentiating Content By differentiating content the standards are met while the needs of the particular students being taught are considered. The teacher strategically selects the information to teach and the best resources with which to teach it using different genres, leveling materials, using a variety of instructional materials, and providing choice.

Differentiating Assessment Tools Most teachers already differentiate assessment during and after the learning. However, it is equally important to assess what knowledge or interests students bring to the learning formally or informally.

Assessing student knowledge prior to the learning experience helps the teacher find out:

- What standards, objectives, concepts, skills the students already understand

- What further instruction and opportunities for mastery are needed

- What areas of interests and feelings will influence the topic under study

- How to establish flexible groups—total, alone, partner, small group

Differentiating Performance Tasks In a differentiated classroom, the teacher provides various opportunities and choices for the students to show what they've learned. Students use their strengths to show what they know through a reflection activity, a portfolio, or an authentic task.

Differentiating Instructional Strategies When teachers vary instructional strategies and activities, more students learn content and meet standards. By targeting diverse intelligences and learning styles, teachers can develop learning activities that help students work in their areas of strength as well as areas that still need strengthening.

Some of these instructional strategies include:

- Graphic organizers

- Cubing

- Role-playing

- Centers

- Choice boards

- Adjustable assignments

- Projects

- Academic contracts

When planning, teachers in the differentiated classroom focus on the standards, but also adjust and redesign the learning activities, tailoring them to the needs of the unique learners in each classroom. Teachers also consider how the brain operates and strive to use research-based, best practices to maximize student learning. Through differentiation we give students the opportunity to learn to their full potential. A differentiated classroom engages students and facilitates learning so all learners can succeed!

CHAPTER 1

Mathematics

Calendar Fun

Standard
Measurement—Understand measurable attributes of objects and the units, systems, and processes of measurement.

Strategies
Rehearsal

Sponge activity

Objective
Students will review facts about the calendar.

Fill transition times during instruction with a special challenge your students will enjoy. In this compelling sponge activity, students review their knowledge of the months of the year.

1. Teach the following chant to students.
   Don't be late.
   Can you state
   A fact or a date
   For _____? (name of a month)

2. Have all students remain in their seats except for the leader. Invite the leader to walk around the room while reciting the chant and naming a month.

3. After completing the chant, the leader continues to walk around the room while counting to 20. This gives students time to think of an answer to the chant. At 20, the leader chooses a student to answer the chant by tapping him or her on the shoulder. The chosen student must state a fact for that month. For example, *November has 30 days; Thanksgiving takes place;* or *it is the fall season.*

4. If the answer is correct, that student takes the leader's place. If the answer is incorrect, the leader continues. Establish a rule that a month can be repeated, but students' answers cannot.

Ideas for More Differentiation
Post the chant to reinforce words for linguistic learners. Support students who need interpersonal interaction by having the group chant with them.

Choose Your Coins

Standard

Measurement—Understand measurable attributes of objects and the units, systems, and processes of measurement.

Objective

Students will use coins to represent different money amounts.

Materials

Count Your Coins reproducible
coin manipulatives
books

This game for two players encourages interpersonal learners to share their knowledge and reinforces logical mathematical thinking.

1. Pair up students by assigning partners of varied skill levels. Give each pair a copy of the **Count Your Coins reproducible (page 11)** and some coin manipulatives. Invite students to cut apart the cards.

2. Have each pair place their cards facedown in a pile between them. Instruct students to place a book standing up between them in order to hide their work areas from one another. Have students turn over the top card and read the amount written on it. Challenge students to use the coin manipulatives to represent the amount of money on the card. Explain that in order to win a point, each team member must use a different combination of coins.

3. When both students have selected coins to represent the amount, tell them to remove the book and look at one another's work. If they succeeded in representing the amount in two different ways, their team earns a point. After ten rounds, ask pairs to share their scores to see which is the winning team.

Ideas for More Differentiation

Invite intrapersonal learners, who work best independently, to complete the activity on their own, representing each card's amount in two different ways.

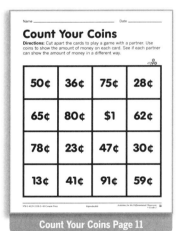

Count Your Coins Page 11

Count Your Coins

Directions: Cut apart the cards to play a game with a partner. Use coins to show the amount of money on each card. See if each partner can show the amount of money in a different way.

50¢	36¢	75¢	28¢
65¢	80¢	$1	62¢
78¢	23¢	47¢	30¢
13¢	41¢	91¢	59¢

Reach Your Goal!

Standard
Numbers and Operations—Understand numbers, ways of representing numbers, relationships among numbers, and number systems.

Objective
Students will develop concepts about place value by using a calculator to determine ways to reach a target number.

Materials
Reach Your Goal! reproducible
calculators
overhead calculator (optional)

Students need varied activities to develop and reinforce an understanding of place value. If they use a calculator to add *1* repeatedly, they can see how the ones digit changes each time and the tens digit changes less frequently. This calculator activity challenges students to begin at one number and work to reach a goal number.

Reach Your Goal! Page 13

1. Have students work in pairs. Give each pair a calculator and a copy of the **Reach Your Goal! reproducible (page 13)**. Use an overhead calculator, if one is available, to demonstrate this activity.

2. Provide students with a starting number, such as *59*. Instruct them to add or subtract to reach *75*. Tell students they are not allowed to press the *clear* button on the calculator. Suggest that one student add or subtract on the calculator while a partner writes down each number added or subtracted. This strategy encourages students to use different approaches to reach the goal number. They decide if they will add or subtract ones or tens. There are many ways to reach the goal number.

3. With students, read aloud the instructions on the reproducible page. Partners can switch roles after each goal number is reached.

4. Invite pairs to share some of the ways they reached their goals with the rest of the class. Point out how they thought about place value in their approaches.

Ideas for More Differentiation
Pair students by ability, and invite them to take turns giving each other a starting number and a goal number.

Reach Your Goal!

Directions: Start with the first number on the chart. Use a calculator to add or subtract numbers until you reach the number in the next row. (Do not press the clear button.) Continue until you reach the number in the last row, writing all the numbers you add or subtract.

Number	What numbers did you add or subtract?
90	
70	
40	
39	
4	

Number	What numbers did you add or subtract?
87	
57	
37	
137	
138	

Number	What numbers did you add or subtract?
99	
113	
123	
83	
89	

Number	What numbers did you add or subtract?
110	
100	
55	
25	
28	

Making Patterns

Standard

Algebra—Understand patterns, relations, and functions.

Objective

Students will follow directions to create and extend patterns.

Materials

Make a Pattern reproducible

small, resealable plastic bags

scissors, tape

small objects (buttons, paperclips, bottle caps, nuts, bolts, washers, screws, acorns, dried beans, pennies)

Combine a math concept with a tactile experience, and you've got lots of learning fun with real-world objects! In this activity, students make patterns, predictions, and discoveries using hands-on materials.

1. Ahead of time, gather several different kinds of small objects. Place each group of objects in a small resealable plastic bag. Prepare enough bags so that the class will have one bag of each object per three or four students.

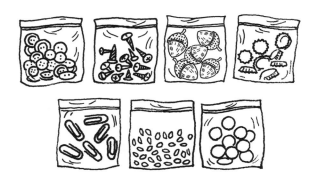

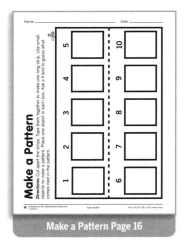

Make a Pattern Page 16

2. Give students a copy of the **Make a Pattern reproducible (page 16)**. Have students cut the page into two strips and tape the pieces together to form one long strip with the numbers in order from 1 to 10.

3. Give instructions for making patterns with the objects, and ask students to complete the patterns. For example, have students place a button in box 1, an acorn in box 2, a washer in box 3, a button in box 4, and an acorn in box 5.

Ask students: *What should go in box #6?* After several practices, ask students to project beyond the sequence shown on their paper strips, for example: *What should go in box #20?*

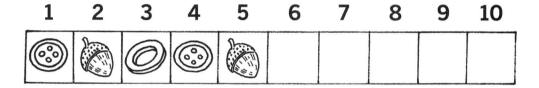

| 1 | 2 | 3 | 4 | 5 | 6 | 7 | 8 | 9 | 10 |

4. Ask students to invent their own patterns in the same manner. Choose volunteers to give instructions to the class for making a pattern. Invite other students to guess what will come next.

Ideas for More Differentiation

Invite students to work in pairs. One student places objects in a pattern. His or her partner is blindfolded and tries to guess what comes next by feeling the objects without looking at them. For a greater challenge, invite the blindfolded student to find and place the correct object(s) needed to complete the pattern.

Make a Pattern

Directions: Cut apart the strips. Tape them together to make one long strip. Use small objects to make a pattern. Place one object in each box. Ask a friend to guess what comes next in the pattern.

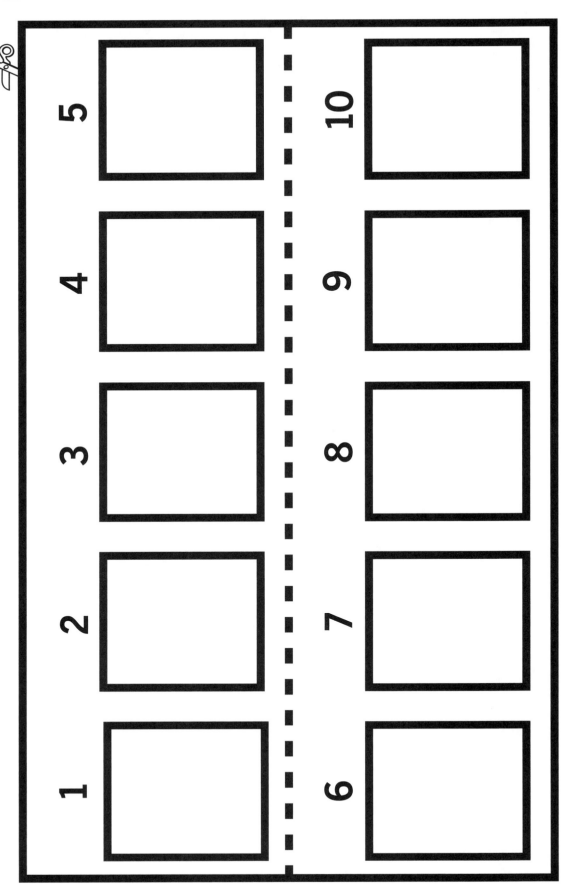

Reproducible

Fun with Shapes

Standard
Geometry—Use visualization, spatial reasoning, and geometric modeling to solve problems.

Objective
Students will manipulate plane figures to make new geometric shapes.

Materials
Making Shapes reproducible
overhead projector
scissors

When learning about geometric properties of shapes, students benefit greatly from hands-on experiences with shape manipulatives. Combining or cutting shapes to make new shapes and recording the results allows students to develop visualization and spatial skills.

1. Give students a copy of the **Making Shapes reproducible (page 18)**. Ask students to identify each pair of shapes at the bottom of the page. Have them cut out the square and triangle. Explain that these make one set of shapes. The two right triangles make another set.

2. Using an overhead projector, have several students demonstrate a new shape that can be made with the square and triangle. Trace around each new shape so the outline remains for comparison with other new shapes.

3. Have the class make the same new shapes and draw them in the left column of their papers. Invite students to complete the right column independently, using the two right triangles to create and draw shapes.

Ideas for More Differentiation
Challenge students to categorize the new shapes and compare them, noting their similarities and differences. Invite them to use a graphic organizer to sort the shapes by number of sides, number of corners, or symmetry.

Making Shapes

Directions: Cut out the shapes at the bottom of the page. Use them to make new shapes. Draw the new shapes in the columns.

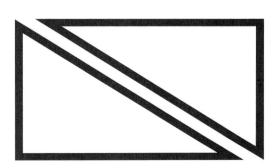

Pockets, Pockets, Pockets

Standard
Data Analysis and Probability—Formulate questions that can be addressed with data, and collect, organize, and display relevant data to answer them.

Objective
Students will organize data on a graph and discover the mode.

Materials
Counting Pockets reproducible
index cards
bulletin board paper

Second graders need to develop skills in formulating questions for exploring information, organizing responses, and representing data collected. Nurture their natural inquisitiveness with an activity about pockets—not what is in them but how many they and their classmates are wearing!

1. Initiate a class discussion by asking students: *Who is wearing the most pockets today? Who is wearing the fewest pockets?* Give students an opportunity to count and report the number of pockets they have. *How many pockets do most students in our class have today?* As students are counting, lead them to conclude that they need a strategy to keep track of all the pockets.

2. Distribute index cards to students, and have them write the number of pockets they are wearing. Collect all the cards, and ask: *How can we organize our data to find out the number of pockets most students are wearing today?* Lead students to conclude that they can sort the cards by number to organize them.

3. Explain that graphs can be used to organize and show data. Suggest that making a graph can help the class show their data about pockets. Make a class graph using bulletin board paper. Show a vertical axis with the number of students and a horizontal axis with the number of pockets.

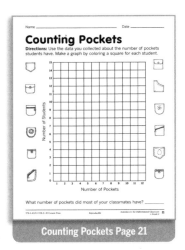

4. Invite students to come to the graph one by one and tape their index cards to the graph.

5. Give students a copy of the **Counting Pockets reproducible (page 21)**. Invite them to transfer the data from the class graph to this page by coloring the appropriate boxes in the grid.

6. Lead students to conclude that by using the graph, they can easily see which number of pockets occurs most frequently.

Ideas for More Differentiation

- Teach the term *mode* to more advanced students. The *mode* is the value that occurs most often in a set of data. Invite these students to determine the mode for the data in the graph.

- Have students work in small groups to count and graph other classroom objects, such as buttons or zippers on students' clothing. They can also graph number of pets, types of pets, favorite kinds of books (by genre), favorite foods, hair and eye color, and more.

Counting Pockets

Directions: Use the data you collected about the number of pockets students have. Make a graph by coloring a square for each student.

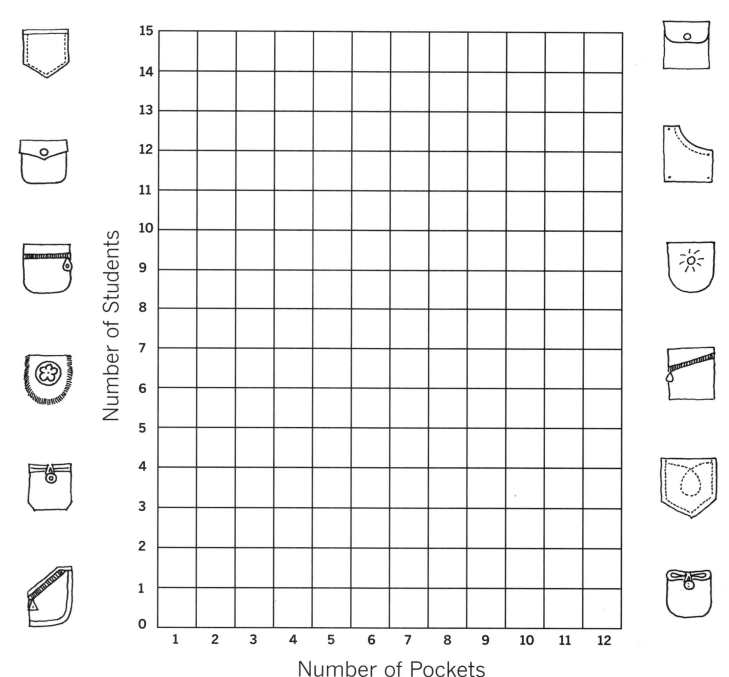

What number of pockets did most of your classmates have? _____

Can You Feel Time Pass?

Standard

Measurement—Understand measurable attributes of objects and the units, systems, and processes of measurement.

Objective

Students will estimate the passing of time.

Materials

An Hour or a Minute? reproducible
digital timer

This focus activity helps students develop a sense of time using their kinesthetic strengths.

1. Use a digital timer for this activity. (Using a manual timer that ticks can be a distraction. If a timer is not available, use a clock with a second hand and a triangle or bell to signal the end of the time period.)

2. Tell students you will set the timer for 30 seconds. Have them stand in an open space with their backs to you and their eyes closed. Tell them to slowly bend their knees into a squat, touching the floor when the timer rings. They will judge how quickly to move.

3. Repeat this 30-second activity several times to give students an opportunity to refine their time estimates and the speed at which they lower their bodies to the ground.

4. Tell students the time period will now change, but don't tell them whether you are changing the time period to be shorter or longer. Set your timer for 15 seconds, and have students repeat the motion. Ask: *Was this time period shorter or longer than the first?* Give students several opportunities to match their movement to the new time.

5. Repeat this activity on subsequent days, comparing different lengths of time to help students refine their sense of duration. Give students a copy of the **An Hour or a Minute? reproducible (page 23)**. Invite them to determine if each activity can best be completed in one minute or one hour. Ask students to name other activities, such as brushing their teeth, that can be done in one minute.

An Hour or a Minute? Page 23

An Hour or a Minute?

Directions: Write **hour** or **minute** under each picture to show about how long each activity would take to complete.

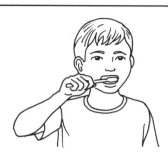

Brush your teeth

_____

Play softball

_____

Wash your hands

_____

Watch a talent show

_____

Plant a garden

_____

Shop for food

_____

Eat a cookie

_____

Sharpen pencils

_____

Feed fish

_____

Draw Me a Picture

Strategies

Problem-based learning

After-learning assessment

Standard

Problem Solving—Solve problems that arise in mathematics and in other contexts.

Objective

Students will draw pictures to solve mathematical problems.

Materials

Art Show reproducible

Drawing pictures is a concrete, problem-solving strategy that can help young learners visualize a word problem. This activity asks students to solve problems by representing relevant data with pictures.

Art Show Page 25

1. Give students two copies of the **Art Show reproducible (page 25)**. Explain that you will give them a problem to solve, and they will use the picture frames to solve it.

2. Write the first problem on the board. Explain that the first step to solving a problem is to ask: *What do I know?* Discuss how to solve the problem with pictures. *How many picture frames will we need? What should we draw?* Solve the problem together with students.

   Problem 1
   Kayla liked the animal paintings she saw in the art show. There were three dogs, two kittens, and a lion. The first painting had a dog and a kitten. The second one had two dogs. The third painting was her favorite. What animals were in it?

3. Write the second problem on the board. Encourage students to solve it independently by drawing pictures. This activity will help you assess the need for further instruction or practice in drawing pictures to solve problems.

   Problem 2
   Alan painted three portraits of the five people in his family. The first painting showed his mother and father. The second painting showed his twin brothers. How many people were in the third painting?

Ideas for More Differentiation

Encourage students to develop their own word problems and ask classmates to solve them.

Art Show

Directions: Listen to your teacher. Draw pictures to solve the problem.

My answer:

_____

_____

_____

_____

_____

_____

_____

Counting Puzzle

Strategy

Multiple intelligences

Standard

Communication—Organize and consolidate mathematical thinking through communication.

Objective

Students will use various tools to explore counting by even and odd numbers.

Materials

Hundred Chart reproducible
calculators
math counters

Students should be able to use language to communicate mathematical ideas. Language helps them organize and clarify their thinking. This exploratory task helps students communicate with each other about mathematics.

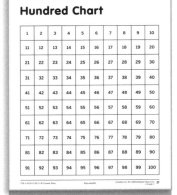

Hundred Chart Page 27

1. Assign students to work in pairs or triads on this task. Give each group a copy of the **Hundred Chart reproducible (page 27)**, calculators, paper and pencils, and counters.

2. Ask students to use their tools to count by 2s to 100. Students may choose to color in every other number on a hundreds chart, repeatedly add 2 on a calculator, count counters two at a time, or use paper and pencil to write numbers. Invite students to explain their strategies.

3. Ask students to count by 3s to 100. Ask students: *Did you end up exactly on 100? Why is that?* Encourage students to use a different tool or method to discover what happens when counting by 3s. Have the class share their discoveries about even and odd numbers by writing their results.

Ideas for More Differentiation

Challenge students with logical/mathematical strengths to predict what will happen when counting by 4s and 5s. Invite them to use the same tools to test their predictions.

Hundred Chart

1	2	3	4	5	6	7	8	9	10
11	12	13	14	15	16	17	18	19	20
21	22	23	24	25	26	27	28	29	30
31	32	33	34	35	36	37	38	39	40
41	42	43	44	45	46	47	48	49	50
51	52	53	54	55	56	57	58	59	60
61	62	63	64	65	66	67	68	69	70
71	72	73	74	75	76	77	78	79	80
81	82	83	84	85	86	87	88	89	90
91	92	93	94	95	96	97	98	99	100

Seasonal Favorites

Strategies

Focus activity

Authentic task

Standard

Earth and Space Science—Understand changes in the earth and sky.

Objective

Students will focus on the differences in the seasons, decide on their favorite seasons, and make a tally chart.

Materials

Favorite Seasons reproducible
individual whiteboards or paper

Students become actively involved in collecting and representing data when it is relevant to their own experiences. In this focus activity, they determine their favorite season and those of their classmates.

1. Write the names of the four seasons on the board. Tell students a riddle about each season. Invite them to guess which season each riddle describes and write their answers on individual whiteboards or paper. Ask students to hold up their answers.

   Tiny flakes touch my nose,
   A cold wind blows and blows.
   What season is it?
   (Answer: *winter*)

   The sun is hot and days are long,
   Then crickets sing a nighttime song.
   What season is it?
   (Answer: *summer*)

Rain makes grass grow green today.
Baby lambs run out to play.
What season is it?
(Answer: *spring*)

Fallen leaves red, yellow, and brown
Dance about upon the ground.
What season is it?
(Answer: *fall*)

2. Give students a copy of the **Favorite Seasons reproducible (page 30)**. After reviewing the seasons, invite students to make a tally chart by interviewing ten of their classmates and recording a tally mark by each classmate's favorite season.

3. After completing the survey, have students circle the season with the most tallies and underline the season with the fewest tallies. Encourage them to share their results with the class.

▶

Favorite Seasons Page 30

Ideas for More Differentiation

Invite auditory learners to work in pairs to verbally compose a riddle about the seasons and recite it to the class. Invite more advanced students to write riddles about the seasons to share.

Favorite Seasons

Directions: Ask your classmates to name their favorite seasons. Make tally marks to show their answers. Circle the season with the most tallies. Draw a line under the season with the fewest tallies.

Spring	
Summer	
Fall	
Winter	

Reproducible 978-1-4129-5338-2 • © Corwin Press

Parts of a Plant

Standard
Life Science—Understand organisms and environments.

Objective
Students will collect plant specimens and use a graphic organizer to classify the parts of a plant.

Materials
Parts of a Plant reproducible
plant parts
basket or tub
heavy construction paper
glue or tape

Delight your naturalist students by encouraging them to closely observe the natural environment while learning about parts of a plant.

1. Begin by discussing the parts of a plant—roots, stems, flowers (fruits, seeds), and leaves. Invite students to bring in plant parts from home or neighborhood. They will most likely find leaves; but encourage them to find other plant parts, such as stems, seeds, fruit, and flowers. (Spring usually yields the greatest plant variety and is the best time to try this activity.) Caution students not to disturb plants without asking permission. Collect their plant parts in a basket or tub.

2. Divide the class into groups of four. Reproduce the **Parts of a Plant reproducible (page 32)** on heavy paper, and give one copy to each group. Have each group glue or tape plant parts from the class collection to each labeled section of the graphic organizer. If they do not have a part, they may draw it.

If the reproducible squares are too small for certain plant parts, have students cut out the squares and glue them to sheets of construction paper. Have them glue their plant parts to the construction paper pages and bind them together to make a booklet.

Ideas for More Differentiation
Have the class arrange the remaining plant parts into a plant-shaped collage on bulletin board paper. Have them draw roots and glue or tape the other parts. They can label roots, stems, fruits, seeds, flowers, and leaves. Ask students to think of a name for their extraordinary plant.

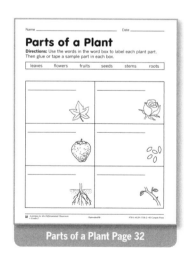

Parts of a Plant Page 32

Name _____ Date _____

Parts of a Plant

Directions: Use the words in the word box to label each plant part.
Then glue or tape a sample part in each box.

| leaves | flowers | fruits | seeds | stems | roots |

It's a Frog's Life

Standard

Life Science—Understand life cycles of organisms.

Objective

Students will create a diagram to depict the life cycle of a frog.

Materials

Life Cycle of a Frog reproducible
nonfiction books about frogs
chart paper
construction paper
scissors, glue

Life cycles are a natural part of the second-grade curriculum. This activity will help students understand the life cycle of a common pond animal, the frog. Challenge students to use their visual/spatial intelligence to create a diagram that depicts the life cycle of a frog.

1. Share with students some nonfiction books about frogs and their life cycle.
   Frog: Watch Me Grow by Lisa Magloff
   From Tadpole to Frog by Wendy Pfeffer
   Life Cycle of a Frog by Bobbie Kalman
   Growing Frogs by Vivian French

2. Draw upon students' prior knowledge and the information they gleaned from the books you shared to brainstorm the life cycle of a frog together. Record their ideas on chart paper.

3. Have students work with a partner. If possible, pair up students of different readiness levels so they can help each other analyze, organize, and remember the information they have learned.

Life Cycle of a Frog.

Female frogs lay their eggs in water.
Frog eggs are small and black.
Jelly around the eggs protects the eggs.
A tadpole pushes out of the egg.

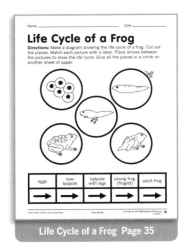

4. Give each student pair a copy of the **Life Cycle of a Frog reproducible (page 35)** and a large sheet of construction paper. Instruct students to cut out the pictures, labels, and arrows and decide together how to arrange them to create a circular diagram that shows the stages of a frog's life. Then have them number the circles in order and glue the pieces in place on the construction paper.

Ideas for More Differentiation

Some students may make a simplified diagram using only three stages—egg, tadpole, and adult frog. More advanced writers may write a description of each stage beneath each picture.

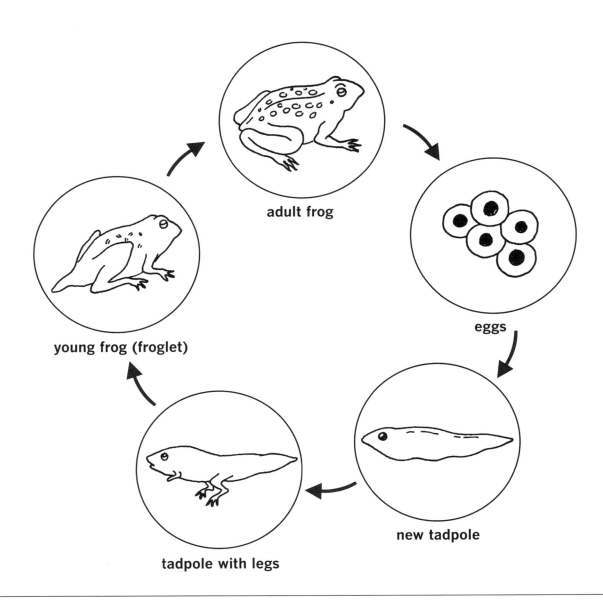

adult frog

eggs

new tadpole

tadpole with legs

young frog (froglet)

Name _____   Date _____

Life Cycle of a Frog

Directions: Make a diagram showing the life cycle of a frog. Cut out the pieces. Match each picture with a label. Place arrows between the pictures to show the life cycle. Glue all the pieces in a circle on another sheet of paper.

eggs	new tadpole	tadpole with legs	young frog (froglet)	adult frog
→	→	→	→	→

The Truth About Talking

Standard
Life Science—Understand characteristics of organisms.

Objective
Students will build a model of the human vocal mechanism.

Materials
How We Talk reproducible
How You Talk by Paul Showers
plastic cups, drinking straws
rubber bands
scissors, glue

Students will discover characteristics of their own vocal mechanism by building a simple model of vocal cords. Building a model is an effective means of authentic assessment that can be used to determine students' understanding.

1. Read aloud the book *How You Talk*, which provides easily understandable information about how lungs, larynx, mouth, nose, lips, tongue, and teeth work together to produce sounds when we talk.

2. Give each student a plastic cup, drinking straw, and two or three rubber bands of different widths. Help students place the rubber bands around the cup so they stretch across the opening. This makes a model of human vocal cords.

3. Ask students what they know about vocal cords. Explain that vocal cords make sounds when air from the lungs passes over them. Have students use their straws to blow forcefully across the rubber bands to make sounds.

4. Give students a copy of the **How We Talk reproducible (page 37)**. Invite them to cut out the labels and glue them on the diagram to demonstrate their understanding of the body parts that help us talk.

How We Talk Page 37

Ideas for More Differentiation
Have students work with a partner and listen to each other's vocal cord models. Ask them: *Do all voices sound alike?* Invite students to think of ways to change the pitch (highness or lowness) of their models.

Name _____   Date _____

How We Talk

Directions: Cut out the labels. Glue them in place to make a diagram showing the body parts that help us talk.

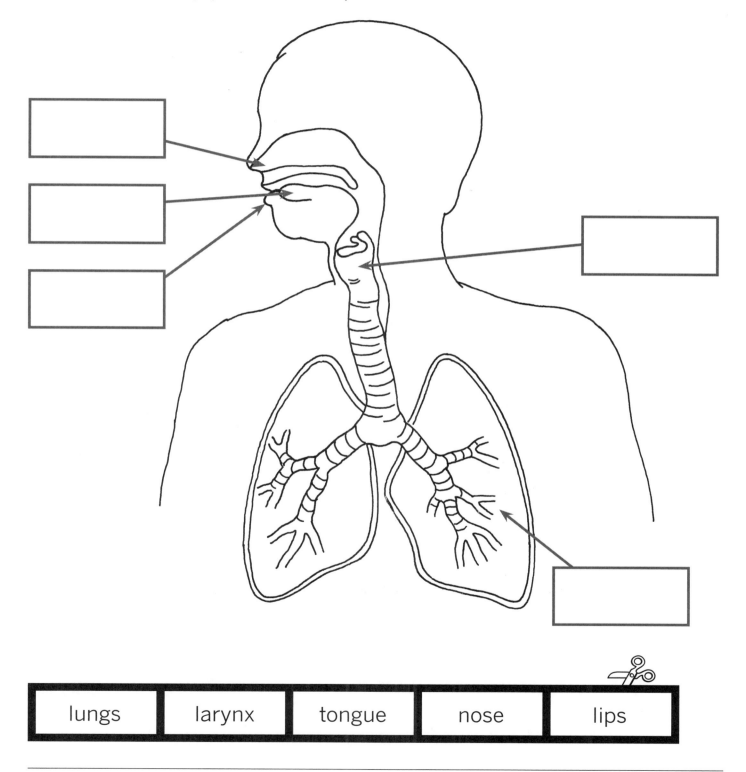

| lungs | larynx | tongue | nose | lips |

Float or Sink

Strategies

Cooperative group learning

Graphic organizer

Standard

Physical Science—Understand properties of objects and materials.

Objective

Students will experiment to see how many marbles float in boats of different sizes.

Materials

Fun with Boats reproducible
aluminum foil
marbles or stones
dishpans of water

Provide the opportunity for students to experiment with objects that float and sink. This tactile experience will broaden students' understanding of the properties of water.

1. Provide each group of four students with a dishpan of water, three different-sized pieces of aluminum foil, a container of marbles or marble-sized stones, and a copy of the **Fun with Boats reproducible (page 39)**.

2. Introduce the lesson by having students drop a marble or stone into their dishpan. What does it do? (*It sinks.*) Ask students if they can think of a way to make the marble float using a piece of foil. Lead them to conclude that they can make a small boat from a piece of foil to carry a load of marbles.

3. Invite students to fashion three different-sized boats with edges all the way around. Have students count the number of marbles each boat can hold before it sinks. Have them record their findings on the reproducible. Encourage students to draw conclusions about the relationship between the size of the boat and the number of marbles that will float.

Ideas for More Differentiation

Challenge students to experiment with other small objects, such as paper clips or pennies. Have students compare their findings with the marble experiment. They can experiment with boat design and shape to improve buoyancy.

Fun with Boats

Directions: Use foil to make three boats of different sizes. How many marbles will each boat hold before it sinks? Complete the chart.

Boat	Tally	Total Marbles
Small		
Medium		
Large		

We found out that _____

Fun with Boats Page 39

Name _____ Date _____

Fun with Boats

Directions: Use foil to make three boats of different sizes. How many marbles will each boat hold before it sinks? Complete the chart.

Boat	Tally	Total Marbles
Small		
Medium		
Large		

We found out that _____

_____

_____

Rocks Are Different

Strategies
Focus activity

Graphic organizer

Standard
Physical Science—Understand properties of objects and materials.

Objective
Students will observe and record descriptions of different kinds of rocks.

Materials
Looking at Rocks reproducible
rocks of various sizes, shapes, and colors
magnifying glasses

Use this focus activity to help students develop the ability to make careful observations as they investigate the properties of rocks.

1. Pair students with partners, and give each pair two copies of the **Looking at Rocks reproducible (page 41)**. Ask students to think of words that describe rocks. Have them write the word *rock* in the center of the web and write descriptive words in the surrounding ovals. Ask pairs to share their words with the class.

2. Display a collection of rocks in various sizes, shapes, and colors. Students may contribute found rocks to the collection.

3. Invite each pair to choose a rock and examine it closely with a magnifying glass. To stimulate students' thinking, ask questions such as: *How would you describe the rock? Does it have patterns? Is it all one material? Is it made up of smaller parts? Close your eyes and feel it. Is it rough, smooth, or both?*

4. Ask students to use the second Looking at Rocks reproducible to describe their chosen rock. Have them draw a picture of their rock in the center of the page and write words that describe their rock in the surrounding ovals.

Ideas for More Differentiation
Students with naturalist intelligence enjoy spending time outdoors. Have these students look for rocks at school or at home. Challenge them to find small rocks, rocks that are too heavy to lift, and rocks that are bigger than themselves. Ask them to draw pictures of the rocks they find. Students with visual/spatial talents can draw pictures of rocks and add a drawing of an object next to each rock to give an idea of its size.

Looking at Rocks Page 41

Looking at Rocks

Directions: Listen to your teacher's directions.
Use this page to describe a rock.

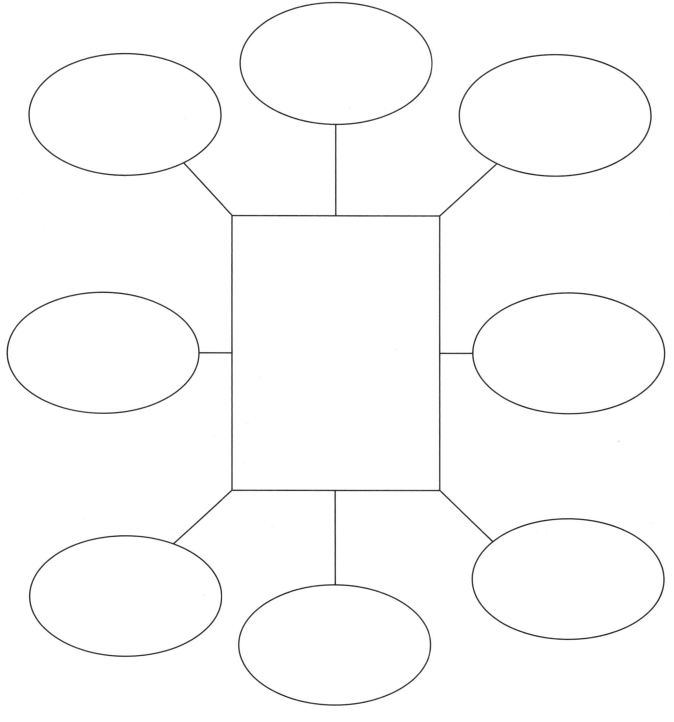

Learning About Dinosaurs

Strategies

Graphic organizer

Authentic task

Standard

Life Science—Understand organisms and environments.

Objective

Students will gather and record data about dinosaurs.

Materials

Dinosaur Graph reproducible
books and online resources about dinosaurs
chart paper

During your study of dinosaurs, guide students to collect information and organize it for purposes of comparison. This authentic activity allows students to gather and record data on dinosaur measurements.

1. Share books and online resources with students to familiarize them with the diversity of dinosaurs and how scientists study them.

   1,001 Facts About Dinosaurs by Neil Clark
   Dinosaur Mummies: Beyond Bare-Bone Fossils by Kelly Milner Halls
   Giant Dinosaurs of the Jurassic by Gregory Wenzel
   National Geographic Dinosaurs by Paul Barrett

2. Begin a class chart by recording the names and lengths of dinosaurs as you read together.

3. Give students a copy of the **Dinosaur Graph reproducible (page 43)**. Beside each dinosaur's name, have students color in the number of squares to indicate its length. Have them add other dinosaur names and lengths to complete the graph.

4. Invite students to compare their graphs in small groups.

Ideas for More Differentiation

Invite students with logical/mathematical abilities to measure and label dinosaur lengths on a playground or other paved area. Have them draw a line with chalk to represent each dinosaur's length.

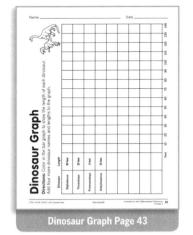

Dinosaur Graph Page 43

Dinosaur Graph

Directions: Color in the bar graph to show the length of each dinosaur. Add four more dinosaur names and lengths to the graph.

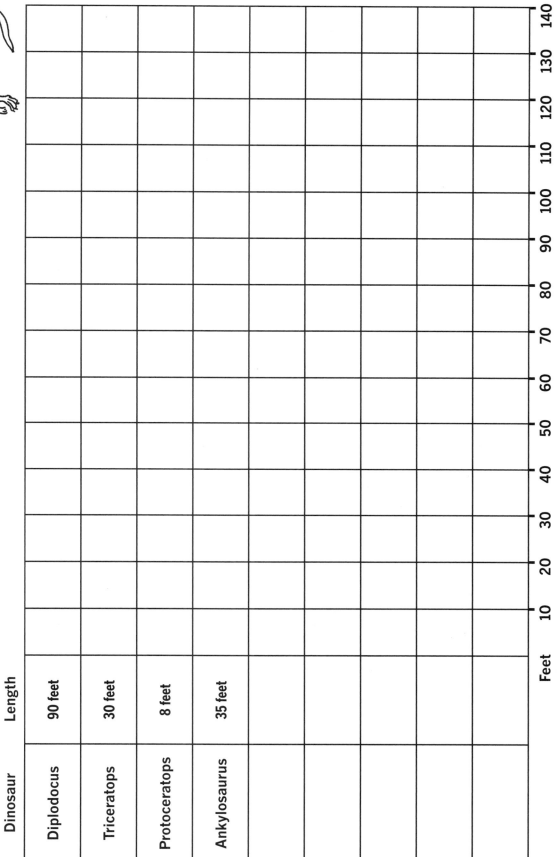

Dinosaur	Length	10	20	30	40	50	60	70	80	90	100	110	120	130	140
Diplodocus	90 feet														
Triceratops	30 feet														
Protoceratops	8 feet														
Ankylosaurus	35 feet														
		Feet													

Where We Get Food

Standard
Science in Personal and Social Perspectives—Identify types of resources.

Objective
Students will illustrate the steps in getting food from farm to table.

Materials
How We Get Our Food reproducibles
paper grocery bag
breakfast food items or containers
various "farm to table" books

Reinforce students' understanding that most food comes from farms, either as crops or as animals that eat crops.

1. Prepare a grocery bag with several breakfast foods or containers, such as a cereal box, a milk carton, a slice of bread, and fruit.

2. Ask students: *Did anyone eat seeds for breakfast this morning?* Show students the items in the bag, and ask them to explain how each came from seeds. For example, grains produce cereal and breads; milk comes from cows that eat grass or hay (that grows from seeds); juice comes from fruit that grows from seeds.

3. Discuss the "farm to table" process.

   From Milk to Ice Cream by Kristin Thoennes Keller
   From Oranges to Orange Juice by Kristin Thoennes Keller
   From Wheat to Bread by Kristin Thoennes Keller

4. Make a class list of the steps involved in food production, including preparing the land, sowing seeds, watering fields, harvesting the food, moving it from the fields, processing it, selling it, storing it, preparing it, and eating it.

5. Give students a copy of the **How We Get Our Food reproducibles (pages 45–46)**. Have them illustrate each step to make a booklet.

How We Get Our Food Page 45

Ideas for More Differentiation
Reinforce the idea that growing food is a process. Sing the song "Oats, Peas, Beans, and Barley Grow" which describes how a farmer sows, waters, weeds, and harvests his crop. Find the song at the Agriculture in the Classroom Web site:
www.agclassroom.org/teacher/pdf/prairie/prek_1/song.pdf.

How We Get Our Food 1

✂

How We Get Our Food

Name: _____

Get the land ready.   1

Sow the seeds.   2

Water the plants.   3

Harvest the food.   4

Move it from the fields.   5

How We Get Our Food 2

Process the food.   6

Sell the food.   7

Store the food.   8

Prepare the food.   9

Eat the food.   10

11

Reproducible

CHAPTER 3

Social Studies

Timeline of a Year

Standard
Understand the ways human beings view themselves in and over time.

Objective
Students will sequence holidays and celebrations to produce a timeline of a year.

Materials
Around the Year reproducible
construction paper
scissors, tape, glue

Students who have become familiar with the calendar can transfer their knowledge to a timeline project. This project helps students understand chronological order and the cycle of a year.

1. Review the order of the months with students. Give students a copy of **Around the Year reproducible (page 48)**.

2. Read the page together. Each box represents a month of the year and contains a symbol for a holiday or other special day. Invite students to fill in the missing words and pictures by making a card for their birthday, a special holiday their family celebrates, and two more special days. Have students color and cut apart the boxes.

3. Give each student a few 4-inch wide strips of construction paper. Have students tape them together into one long strip. Direct students to glue the picture boxes onto their strip in the order in which they occur during the year.

4. When students are finished, instruct them to tape the two ends of the strip together to form a circle of the year.

Around the Year Page 48

Ideas for More Differentiation
Have students find and bring in different types of calendars (wall calendars, desk calendars, pocket calendars, day planners) to share with the class. Compare and contrast the different types of calendars.

Name _____   Date _____

Around the Year

Directions: Make a holiday card for your birthday, a special family celebration, and two more special days. Color and cut out the boxes. Glue them on a strip of paper in order. Tape the ends of the strip together to make a circle of the year.

January 1	February 14	March 20 or 21	April 22
New Year's Day	Valentine's Day	1st Day of Spring	Earth Day
May	June 21 or 22	July 4	August
Mother's Day	1st Day of Summer	Independence Day	Friendship Day
September 20 or 21	October 31	November	December 21 or 22
1st Day of Fall	Halloween	Thanksgiving	1st Day of Winter
_____	_____	_____	_____
My Birthday			

Speed Read Challenge

Standard

Understand the ideals, principles, and practices of citizenship in a democratic republic.

Objective

Students will increase reading vocabulary and fluency in social studies content.

Materials

Speedy U.S. Vocabulary reproducible
Speedy Vocabulary reproducible
timer

Strategy
Focus activity

This focus activity boosts students' comprehension of content reading in the social studies. By gaining experience with vocabulary words they will encounter in their reading, students will improve their fluency and comprehension.

1. Give each student a copy of the **Speedy U.S. Vocabulary reproducible (page 51)**. Students will likely encounter these vocabulary words while reading and writing about the United States.

2. Read the list of vocabulary words together as a class. Explain to students that you will time them for 30 seconds as they read to an "elbow partner" (someone who sits next to them). Encourage them to be as accurate in their reading as possible. Their partner will listen and correct them as needed and will help when they don't know a word.

Speedy U.S. Vocabulary Page 51

3. Set the timer for 30 seconds, and tell students to begin reading. When 30 seconds have passed, instruct them to mark an X next to the last word they read. Then have partners switch roles and repeat the activity.

4. This time, encourage students to read further than they did the first time in the same 30-second period. Again, have students mark an X next to the last word they read when the time is up.

5. Repeat the activity several times to give students an opportunity to see improvement. Have them count the number of words they were able to read in 30 seconds.

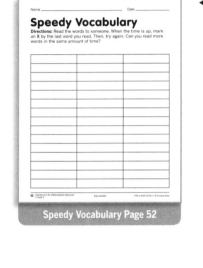

Speedy Vocabulary Page 52

6. Use the **Speedy Vocabulary reproducible (page 52)** to make master copies of vocabulary words drawn from specific chapters or units in your social studies text. Use it as a focus activity before students read a specific chapter or section.

Ideas for More Differentiation

For students who need more challenging words, have them search through library books on the topic you are studying. Encourage them to fill a sheet with as many challenging words as they can find. Students can exchange sheets with each other and use a timer to practice speed-reading the words. Less accomplished readers may benefit from using an index card or bookmark to slide down the page as they read.

Speedy U.S. Vocabulary

Directions: Read the words to someone. When the time is up, mark an **X** by the last word you read. Then, try again. Can you read more words in the same amount of time?

United States	United States	United States
America	America	America
flag	flag	flag
government	government	government
president	president	president
capital	capital	capital
country	country	country
city	city	city
citizen	citizen	citizen
citizenship	citizenship	citizenship
Washington, D.C.	Washington, D.C.	Washington, D.C.
fifty	fifty	fifty
symbol	symbol	symbol
stars	stars	stars
stripes	stripes	stripes

Speedy Vocabulary

Directions: Read the words to someone. When the time is up, mark an **X** by the last word you read. Then, try again. Can you read more words in the same amount of time?

My State

Standard
Understand how people create and change structures of power, authority, and governance.

Objective
Students will demonstrate knowledge of their state by making a state booklet.

Strategies
Multiple intelligences

Structured project

Materials
My State reproducible
books and online resources about your state

California

As students study their state, involve them in creating a project that taps into their visual/spatial abilities and illustrates what they have learned.

1. Ask students to name the number of states in the United States. Make a list of the states students can name. Explain that they are going to make a booklet about their state.

2. Provide books and printed online sources to familiarize students with their state capital, bird, flag, flower, tree, and slogan.

3. Give students a copy of the **My State reproducible (page 54)** to use as a booklet cover. Have students complete the cover by writing the name of their state in the top box and coloring their state on the U.S. map. Students can also indicate where their town is located in their state.

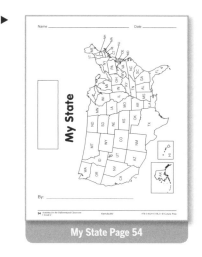

My State Page 54

4. Have students complete their booklets with information about their state. Provide pictures they can use as models for their drawings. Instruct students to do the following: On page 1, write the name of the state capital and draw its location on a state map. On page 2, name and draw the state bird. On page 3, draw the state flag. On page 4, name and draw the state flower. On page 5, name and draw the state tree. On page 6, write and illustrate the state slogan. Add a back cover and bind the booklets with staples, yarn, or ribbon.

Ideas for More Differentiation
Teach students the state song, and have a group of students who learn through musical/rhythmic modalities create movements to accompany it.

Name _____ Date _____

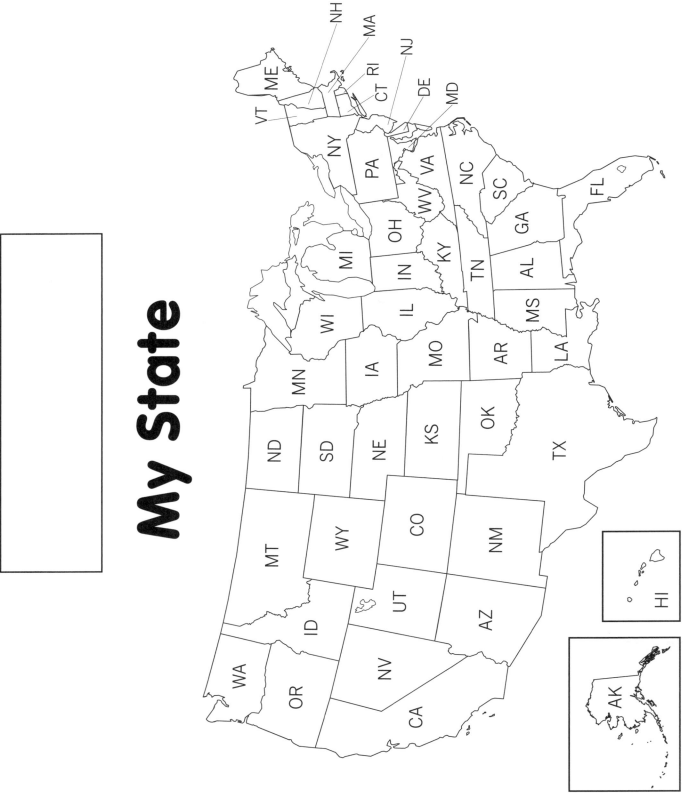

My State

Reproducible

978-1-4129-5338-2 • © *Corwin Press*

By: _____

Transportation

Standard
Understand relationships among science, technology, and society.

Objective
Students will categorize modes of transportation using a graphic organizer.

Materials
Transportation Wheel reproducible
crayons or markers

As students survey the types of transportation their families use, they become aware of the variety of transportation available in their community. In this activity, students use a graphic organizer to categorize modes of transportation.

1. Initiate a class discussion about the places students and their family members travel on a daily basis (grocery store, school) and on a less frequent basis (vacations, visits to faraway relatives). Make a list of modes of transportation students used.

2. Divide the class into groups of four or five students. Give each group a copy of the **Transportation Wheel reproducible (page 56)**.

3. Assign each group a category to write in the center of their graphic organizer: *air, land,* or *water.* Then have groups complete their organizer by drawing or gluing magazine pictures and labeling methods of transportation in that category. For example, for air transportation, students may draw and label an airplane, helicopter, hot air balloon, rocket, and glider. Invite groups to share their ideas with the class.

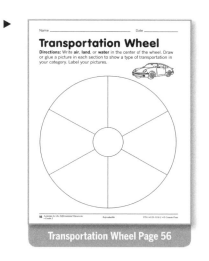

Transportation Wheel Page 56

Ideas for More Differentiation
Students with strong verbal/linguistic abilities can write a story about an imaginary ride they took on the vehicle of their choice. Where did they go? What was the ride like? What did they see and do?

Transportation Wheel

Directions: Write **air**, **land**, or **water** in the center of the wheel. Draw or glue a picture in each section to show a type of transportation in your category. Label your pictures.

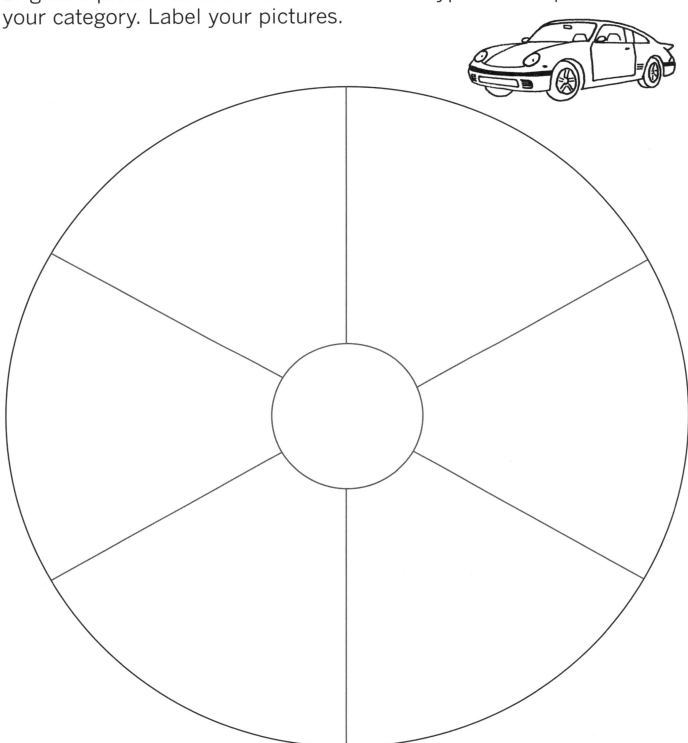

Families Are Alike and Different

Standard
Understand interactions among individuals, groups, and institutions.

Objective
Students will compare families of storybook characters.

Materials
Family Information Chart reproducible
Comparing Families reproducible
books about families

Strategies
Graphic organizer

Bloom's Taxonomy: analysis

Enrich your instruction about families by incorporating literature about different kinds of families. Provide books and the accompanying activities to help students focus on social studies concepts. Use the graphic organizers to enhance students' understanding of family characteristics.

1. Your students may already have experience analyzing their own and others' family trees. To further explore the concept of how families are alike and different, provide books you can read aloud or have students read independently.
   The Best Single Mom in the World by Mary Zisk
   The Chalk Doll by Charlotte Pomerantz
   A Koala for Katie by Jonathan London
   The Little Green Goose by Adele Sansome
   People of the Breaking Day by Marcia Sewall
   There's Only One of Me! by Pat Hutchins

2. Give students a copy of the **Family Information Chart reproducible (page 59)**. After they read one of the selected family stories, show students how to complete the chart. Invite them to list the book title and family members from the story. In the remaining sections of the chart, have students take notes or draw pictures to show how the family's basic needs (e.g., food, housing) are met, what they do for fun, and what traditions they share.

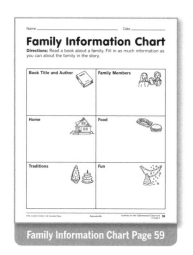

Family Information Chart Page 59

3. After a period of several days, students will have collected a number of Family Information Charts about the books they have read. Tell them they will choose two families to compare similarities and differences.

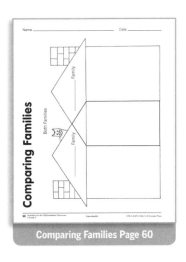

◄ 4. Give students a copy of the **Comparing Families reproducible (page 60)**, and place a transparency of the reproducible on the overhead. Demonstrate how to use this Venn diagram to compare two different families. Point out how to write differences in the two different houses and similarities in the overlapping section between the houses. Invite them to use the reproducible to write or draw their ideas.

5. When they are finished, have students share their Venn diagrams in small groups. They can can work in pairs to compare and contrast their own families. Ask pairs to share information about siblings, pets, family traditions and celebrations, and more.

Ideas for More Differentiation

Have students work with a partner to compare two families using one chart from each of their collections. Invite them to share with the class the resulting Venn diagram they create.

Name _____   Date _____

Family Information Chart

Directions: Read a book about a family. Fill in as much information as you can about the family in the story.

Book Title and Author	Family Members 
Home 	Food 
Traditions 	Fun 

Comparing Families

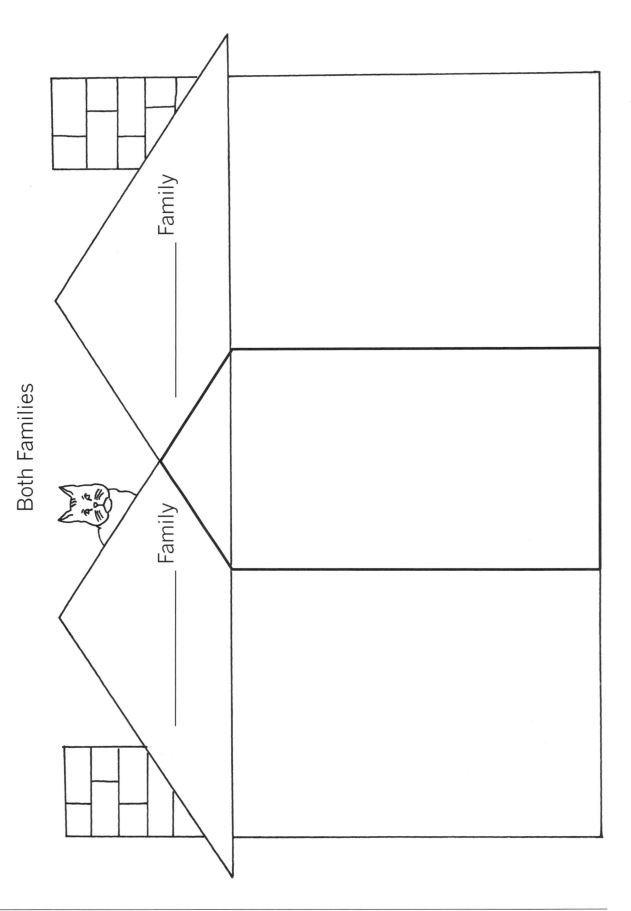

Both Families

Family

Family

In the Right Direction

Standard
Understand the interactions among people, places, and environments.

Objective
Students will explore and practice cardinal directions.

Materials
Compass Rose reproducible
sentence strips
paper plates
scissors, glue

Strategies
Multiple intelligences

Rehearsal

Tap into children's kinesthetic and visual/spatial learning modalities to reinforce basic map skills. This activity will help students learn and remember the cardinal directions.

1. Begin with a movement activity in a large, open space. Write the four directions (*north, south, east,* and *west*) in bold letters on sentence strips. Tape the sentence strips to the walls of the gym or multipurpose room.

2. Have students find their own personal space in the middle of the room. Then ask them to turn and face *north, south, east,* and *west* to familiarize them with the directions.

3. Give instructions that challenge students to move in a particular fashion and in a specific direction, such as: *Skip to the west. Move in slow motion to the north. Do a crab walk to the east. Walk backward to the south. Skate to the west.* Remind students to stay within their own personal space as they follow instructions so they don't collide.

4. To reinforce the movement experience, have students make a compass rose. Give each student a copy of the **Compass Rose reproducible (page 62)** and a paper plate. Demonstrate how to assemble a compass rose by gluing the cutouts onto the plate.

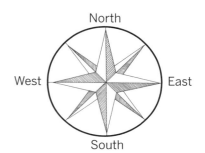

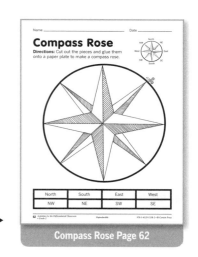

Compass Rose Page 62

Ideas for More Differentiation
Students with verbal/linguistic strengths will enjoy looking at a variety of maps and locating the compass roses. Ask them to list places located in the north, south, east and west regions of their maps.

Compass Rose

Directions: Cut out the pieces and glue them onto a paper plate to make a compass rose.

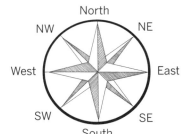

North	South	East	West
NW	NE	SW	SE

America's First People

Standard
Understand culture and cultural diversity.

Objective
Students will create a representation of ancient rock carvings.

Materials
Mesa Verde Designs reproducible
books about ancient civilizations
crayons, markers, colored pencils, scissors
bulletin board paper, tempera paint, spray bottles

As students explore the world of ancient people who lived in America, they will learn about America's cultural roots and cultural diversity. This art project is a way to dig into the past to help students understand people's common desire to create and communicate.

1. Share one or two books about one of America's early civilizations—the Puebloans.

   Ancient Cliff Dwellers of Mesa Verde by Caroline Arnold
   Mesa Verde by Mary Quigley

      Show students examples of the rock art and pottery made by ancestral Puebloan people. Explain that these people did not write words; they carved pictures in rock. They also left hand images, maybe as a way of signing their work.

2. Give each student a copy of the **Mesa Verde Designs reproducible (page 64)**. Invite students to decorate their pots using the design samples and then cut out the pots.

3. Display the decorated pots on bulletin board paper. Invite students to make a handprint next to their pottery design to sign their work. Combine tempera paint and water in a spray bottle. Have students place their hand next to their decorated pot. Have a partner spray their hand and the paper around it. When students lift their hand off the paper, a handprint will remain.

Ideas for More Differentiation
Invite students with visual/spatial talents to experiment with other ways to make handprints and handprint art using a variety of materials.

Mesa Verde Designs Page 64

Mesa Verde Designs

Directions: Practice drawing some ancient designs like those found at Mesa Verde. Decorate the pot, and cut it out.

Workers in Our Community

Standard
Understand how people organize for production, distribution, and consumption of goods and services.

Strategy
Role play

Objective
Students will role-play the interdependence of community workers.

Materials
Community Workers reproducible

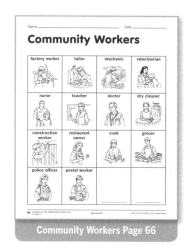

Community Workers Page 66

Build students' awareness of how workers in our community depend on one another. Invite students to participate in this engaging role-play activity to demonstrate this interdependence.

1. Ask the class to help you compile a list of community workers. Talk about the jobs some of those workers perform. Include the workers listed on page 66.

2. Before making copies, add two additional workers unique to your community to the **Community Workers reproducible (page 66)**. Cut apart the squares.

3. Divide students into pairs, and give each student a square with the name of a community worker. Explain to students that they will pretend to be that worker. Ask students to role-play how they might use their partner's services. For example, one student might role-play being a mechanic who takes his dog to the vet for shots. The other student might role-play being a vet who takes her car to the mechanic for an oil change.

4. Encourage students to create scenes to perform for the class. As time permits, collect the cutouts and redistribute new ones for another round.

Ideas for More Differentiation
Encourage interpersonally intelligent students to form groups of three or four to develop longer scenarios involving more community workers.

Community Workers

factory worker	tailor	mechanic	veterinarian
nurse	teacher	doctor	dry cleaner
construction worker	restaurant owner	cook	grocer
police officer	postal worker		

CHAPTER 4

Language Arts

Read Along with Me

Standard

Apply a wide range of strategies to comprehend, interpret, evaluate, and appreciate texts. Draw on prior experience, interactions with other readers and writers, knowledge of word meaning and of other texts, word identification strategies, and understanding of textual features (e.g., sound-letter correspondence, sentence structure, context, graphics).

Strategies
Rehearsal

Authentic task

Objective

Students will read environmental print to search for related words.

Materials

Word Find reproducible

Reading practice in the differentiated classroom isn't always a solitary or a sedentary activity. Encourage students to practice reading print materials in this variation on the classic "read around the room" strategy. This rehearsal activity appeals to students with bodily/kinesthetic and interpersonal learning styles.

1. In the "read around the room" strategy, invite students to practice reading rich sources of environmental text mounted on the classroom walls. To begin, post word charts, lists, word walls, language experience stories, poem and song charts, written reminders, the pledge to the flag, and classroom rules. The materials should constantly be updated, and students should have frequent opportunities to walk around the room with a partner using a pointer to read everything.

2. Structure the activity by providing a list of words for students to find as they read around the room. Write your list of classroom-specific words on the **Word Find reproducible (page 69)** before reproducing it and giving a copy to each student. Have students place a check mark beside each word they find.

3. Invite student pairs to begin at a designated starting place and move around the room following a predetermined course, reading as they go.

Word Find Page 69

To make the strategy even more appealing, be on the lookout for magic wands, festive batons, hand-shaped flyswatters, and light sticks to serve as pointers.

For more fun, create your word lists using current curriculum topics (e.g., *pond, duck, swim*) or holidays and seasons (e.g., *costume, Halloween, boo*). Make a list of rhyming words (e.g., *troll, hole, bowl*) or compound words (e.g., *butterfly, newspaper, playground*). Varying the list weekly will give students many opportunities for word practice.

Ideas for More Differentiation

Some students will be ready for a more challenging activity. Provide blank Word Find reproducibles for students to compile their own lists. Challenge them to find all the color words on the wall or all the words beginning with a digraph (e.g., *sh, ch, th, wh*).

Name _____ Date _____ | Name _____ Date _____

Word Find

Directions: Find these words as you read around the room. Put a check mark in the box next to each word you find.

☐ _____

☐ _____

☐ _____

☐ _____

☐ _____

☐ _____

☐ _____

☐ _____

☐ _____

☐ _____

Word Find

Directions: Find these words as you read around the room. Put a check mark in the box next to each word you find.

☐ _____

☐ _____

☐ _____

☐ _____

☐ _____

☐ _____

☐ _____

☐ _____

☐ _____

☐ _____

Active Listening

Strategies

Role play

Authentic task

Standard

Participate as knowledgeable, reflective, creative, and critical members of a variety of literacy communities.

Objective

Students will role-play good listening audience behaviors.

Materials

Good Audience Behaviors reproducible

When having students recite poetry and give speeches, also include instruction on how to be a good listener. Good listening skills are not only helpful to learning in the classroom, but also in being a good audience member. This role-play activity gives students an opportunity to practice positive audience behaviors.

1. Lead a class discussion about proper audience behaviors. Ask: *When are we invited to be an audience?* (school assemblies, talent shows, plays, classroom speeches). *What can an audience do to help a speaker? What does a good audience look and sound like?*

2. Review the list of behaviors on the **Good Audience Behaviors reproducible (page 71)**, and add ideas specific to your class. Give students a copy of the revised reproducible and review the behaviors.

3. Invite half the class to role-play attending a school assembly or play. They will arrive at the venue, take a seat, sit quietly and politely, listen, applaud, and exit. Have the other half of the class watch and comment on the proper behaviors they saw. Then have groups reverse roles.

4. You may wish to have students keep this list of behaviors in a folder or binder so they can refer to it throughout the year.

Ideas for More Differentiation

Some students need additional help focusing their attention. If you notice students having difficulty during class read-aloud times, give them a lump of clay to manipulate while listening. Direct them to make something from the story.

Good Audience Behaviors Page 71

Name _____   Date _____

Good Audience Behaviors

Looks Like

Walks in and sits down quickly

Sits so others can see

Keeps eyes on speaker

Keeps hands and feet to oneself

Smiles and nods at speaker

_____

_____

_____

Sounds Like

Walks in and sits down quietly

Listens so others can hear

Does not talk to others

Keeps hands and feet quiet

Applauds at the right times

_____

_____

_____

Performing Poetry

Strategies

Authentic task

Multiple intelligences

Standard

Read a wide range of literature from many periods in many genres to build an understanding of the many dimensions (e.g., philosophical, ethical, aesthetic) of human experience.

Objective

Students will perform a poem.

Materials

The Wind reproducible
overhead projector
chart paper
colored markers
highlighter markers

Students need many experiences listening to, reading, and reciting poetry in small and large groups before they are asked to individually perform a poem. This authentic performance task builds on students' musical/rhythmic and verbal/linguistic abilities and provides practice in fluency.

1. Introduce the poem "The Wind" by Robert Louis Stevenson by reading it aloud to the class.

2. Prepare a transparency of **The Wind reproducible (page 74)**, and display ▶ it on an overhead projector. Read the poem aloud a second time.

3. Invite students to tell you about the poem. Prompt them with questions such as: *Who is talking in the poem? What does he wonder about? What does he know about the wind?*

4. Write the poem on chart paper using four different colored markers. Print each verse in a different color and the refrain in a fourth color.

5. Give each student a copy of The Wind reproducible and colored highlighter markers. Have students highlight the verses using colors similar to those on the chart paper.

6. Assign a color to each table, row, or other small group. Have each group practice its part of the poem. Remind students to listen to each other as they read in order to stay together. Challenge them to read expressively with emotion.

7. Read through the entire poem again with each group chiming in at the appropriate place. Encourage students to applaud each other at the end. Comment on things you liked, such as pacing, expression, and clarity.

8. On subsequent days, change the color assignments so students have an opportunity to read all sections of the poem.

Ideas for More Differentiation

Encourage strong readers who enjoy reciting poetry to introduce a poem to the class by reading one line at a time and having the group repeat each line after him or her.

The Wind Page 74

Name _____ Date _____

The Wind

I saw you toss the kites on high
And blow the birds about the sky;
And all around I heard you pass,
Like ladies' skirts across the grass—
    O wind, a-blowing all day long,
    O wind, that sings so loud a song!

I saw the different things you did,
But always you yourself you hid,
I felt you push, I heard you call,
I could not see yourself at all—
    O wind, a-blowing all day long,
    O wind, that sings so loud a song!

O you that are so strong and cold,
O blower, are you young or old?
Are you a beast of field and tree,
Or just a stronger child than me?
    O wind, a-blowing all day long,
    O wind, that sings so loud a song!

Robert Louis Stevenson

Reproducible

Antonyms Are Opposites

Standard
Apply knowledge of language structure, language conventions (e.g., spelling and punctuation), media techniques, figurative language, and genre to create, critique, and discuss print and nonprint texts.

Objective
Students will apply their knowledge of antonyms.

Materials
Name That Book! reproducible
sentence strips, pocket chart

Use this focus activity to develop students' reading vocabulary. Build on students' knowledge of favorite books as they work with antonyms.

1. Guide students to focus on words with opposite meanings. Access prior knowledge by asking students to tell you some word opposites they know. Explain that these are called *antonyms*.

2. Prepare sentence strips with book titles familiar to students. Change a word in each title to its antonym, and underline the word. For example, *Chicken Little* becomes *Chicken Big*, and *The Lion King* becomes *The Lion Queen*. Write the correct antonym that completes each book title on a smaller strip to make word cards.

3. Place the book titles in a pocket chart. Divide the class into small groups, and give each group an antonym word card. Ask a volunteer to read a book title aloud. Invite the group that has the correct antonym card to stand and read their word to the class. Have the class read the title using the new word.

4. Give students a copy of the **Name That Book! reproducible (page 76)**. Invite them to write an antonym for each bold word in the book titles (*Chicken **Little**, The Lion **King**, A Baby **Sister** for Frances, The Relatives **Came**, Clifford the **Big** Red Dog, **Beauty** and the Beast, **Amazing** Grace, Where the **Wild** Things Are, Harry the **Dirty** Dog*).

Ideas for More Differentiation
Have students search the library for book titles they can change. Challenge them to write antonyms for as many book-title words as they can. Then have students read aloud their new titles to see how many the class can guess.

Name That Book! Page 76

Name _____ Date _____

Name That Book!

Directions: Read each book title. Find the antonym in the word box for each bold word. Write the correct title.

Sister	King	Little
Beauty	Big	Wild
Amazing	Came	Dirty

Chicken **Big**

The Lion **Queen**

A Baby **Brother** for Frances

_____

The Relatives **Went**

Clifford the **Little** Red Dog

Ugly and the Beast

_____

Ordinary Grace

Where the **Calm** Things Are

Harry the **Clean** Dog

_____

Sorting Words

Standard

Apply a wide range of strategies to comprehend, interpret, evaluate, and appreciate texts. Draw on prior experience, interactions with other readers and writers, knowledge of word meaning and of other texts, word identification strategies, and understanding of textual features (e.g., sound-letter correspondence, sentence structure, context, graphics).

Strategies
Focus activity

Game

Objective

Students will sort words based on phonetic elements.

Materials

index cards
pocket chart

Word-sorting activities help students closely study word parts and features. Focus activities, such as this word game, are fun to play while building reading vocabulary and word identification skills.

1. Make 12 word cards by writing words from a word wall or story on index cards. Place the word cards in a pocket chart.

2. Distribute 12 index cards to each student. Have him or her make a set of word cards to match the words in the pocket chart.

3. Give students directions on how to sort the cards. You can guide students to focus on a particular word feature, for example: *Find and group the words **run**, **red**, **rug**, and **rest***. Ask students to guess what the words have in common. In this case, they all begin with the letter *r*.

4. You can also have students sort words with the same ending sound or number of letters, silent letters, the same vowel sound, or blends. Structure the activity to support your phonics lessons.

Ideas for More Differentiation

Focus on word meaning by asking students to find words that name things, describe things, or show action. For an extra challenge, have student pairs take turns giving each other sorting criteria.

Biography Salad

Standard

Read a wide range of literature from many periods in many genres to build an understanding of the many dimensions (e.g., philosophical, ethical, aesthetic) of human experience.

Objective

Students will listen (read) for biographical details in biographies.

Materials

Biography Salad reproducible
biographies
green paper, scissors
bowl

Second graders are becoming aware of the larger world and the concept of time. This is a good time to use biographies to introduce them through biographies to the lives and achievements of others. Use this focus activity to help students learn and remember the details of a person's life.

1. Introduce the biography genre by pointing out several biographies students have read or heard. Explain that biographies are nonfiction. They are true stories about real people.

2. Before reading a biography, copy the **Biography Salad reproducible (page 79)** on green paper, and cut apart the cards. Place the cards in a "salad bowl." Invite students to select a card.

3. Select and read aloud a biography. While you read, tell students to listen carefully for the story details on their cards.
   Harriet Tubman and the Freedom Train by Sharon Gayle
   Susan B. Anthony by Deborah Hopkinson
   Thomas Alva Edison by Wil Mara
   Young Orville and Wilbur Wright by Andre Woods

4. When you finish reading, have students place their cards back in the salad bowl one at a time while stating information from the story that corresponds to their card. Invite the class to help by adding details.

Ideas for More Differentiation

Invite students with visual/spatial skills to draw a picture of the person or important things from the story as they listen to the biography.

Biography Salad

Person's name	When born	Where lived
When died	Family members	Kind of work
Childhood dreams	Special talents	Famous for
Liked	Loved	Disliked
Feared	Wanted to	Overcame

Biography Salad Page 79

Biography Salad

Person's name	When born	Where lived
When died	Family members	Kind of work
Childhood dreams	Special talents	Famous for
Liked	Loved	Disliked
Feared	Wanted to	Overcame

Writing About Giants

Strategy
Cooperative group learning

Standard

Employ a wide range of strategies while writing, and use different writing process elements appropriately to communicate with different audiences for a variety of purposes.

Objective

Students will cooperatively write a story together.

Materials

A Giant Story reproducible

Most students are familiar with stories about giants, such as *The Selfish Giant, Jack and the Beanstalk,* and *Clifford the Big Red Dog.* In this cooperative group activity, students will work together to write their own creative giant story.

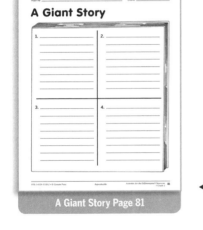

A Giant Story Page 81

1. Remind students of stories about giants they may have heard. List some topics on the board. Then tell an imaginary story about a time when you found a giant egg in your backyard. Invite students to imagine what you did with the egg. Write their ideas on the board, such as: *scrambled eggs for the whole town's breakfast; decorated it and gave it to an art museum; found someone or something big enough to sit on it so it would hatch;* or *made hundreds of egg salad sandwiches.*

2. Divide the class into groups of four, and assign each group member a number from 1 to 4. Give each group a copy of the **A Giant Story reproducible (page 81)**. Assign the groups a topic idea from the list generated on the board.

3. Explain that groups must use all four sections of the paper. Each group member writes one part of the story in a section. Student 1 begins by writing by an opening for the story in the first box. Student 2 writes what happens next in the second box. Student 3 adds to the storyline in the third box, and student 4 writes the conclusion in the fourth box. Invite groups to share their stories.

Ideas for More Differentiation

Some students may work independently on their own giant stories. Provide them with a copy of the reproducible and some suggestions. For example, ask them to craft a story about what they might do with a giant four-leaf clover, a giant ant, or a giant pumpkin.

A Giant Story

1. _____
   _____
   _____
   _____
   _____
   _____
   _____

2. _____
   _____
   _____
   _____
   _____
   _____
   _____

3. _____
   _____
   _____
   _____
   _____
   _____

4. _____
   _____
   _____
   _____
   _____
   _____

CHAPTER 5

Physical Education, Art, and Music

Bubbling in Place

Objective
Students will learn to move in their own personal space.

Materials
drum and mallet

Creative movement activities require students to move in their own personal space without interfering with others. Use this focus activity to help students establish a comfortable personal space as well as respect the personal space of others around them.

1. Use a large, open space for this activity. Explain to students that when everyone is moving in a space, they need to be considerate of others. From where they are standing, invite students to notice the empty spaces in the room.

2. Have students spread out around the room to find their own spot. Each student's spot should be at least an arm's length away from anyone else.

978-1-4129-5338-2

3. Call out a movement, and invite students to make that movement when they hear a drum beat, for example: *Put your arms out to the sides.* (Beat drum.) *Turn around once.* (Beat drum.) *Raise your arms up high.* (Beat drum.) *Bring your arms down, and clap three times.* (Beat drum.) *Freeze.* (Beat drum.)

4. Ask students if they are still standing in their own spot. Have them imagine that they are standing inside a big bubble. The bubble is called their personal space. Tell students they are going to explore the space inside their bubble without moving from their spot.

5. Give students more movement directions, and beat the drum after each direction. For example:
   - *Reach as high as you can inside your bubble. Touch the bubble's ceiling.*
   - *Bring your arms down slowly, and touch the sides of your bubble.*
   - *Reach down as low as you can.*
   - *Feel the bottom of the bubble.*
   - *Without moving from your spot, reach out to the side as far as you can.*
   - *Bend and reach in another direction.*
   - *Stand back up and freeze.*

6. Encourage students to explore the inside of their bubbles without moving from their spots. Play a steady drumbeat as they move. Direct students to freeze in their current positions when the drumbeat stops. Repeat the activity, and have students notice others' freeze positions. Repeat the activity several times.

Ideas for More Differentiation

- After students have grasped the concept of personal space, invite them to move away from their spots and return to them within four to eight drumbeats. Challenge them to move with different motions, such as smooth, jerky, swinging, shaky, slow, or quick.

- Students with bodily/kinesthetic abilities can take the activity even further. Have them work in small groups of four to invent a sequence of movements. Invite students to use four beats for each movement and do them in any order or pattern they wish.

Animals Move

Strategy
Focus activity

Objective
Students will create a movement sequence using animal movements of different qualities.

Materials
animal pictures

Exploring animal movements is a good introductory movement activity. Use this activity to focus students' attention on creating movement that helps them communicate.

1. Show students a variety of animal pictures, and discuss different categories of animals they know, such as mammals, birds, reptiles, amphibians, insects, and fish. Point out that some animals have two legs and some have four. Access prior knowledge by asking students to name different animals they know about.

2. Ask students to suggest words that describe how a bird moves (e.g., *gliding, soaring, fluttering, diving*). Direct them to show those movements using their bodies. Ask students to describe other animal movements and then show those movements. Give students time to explore each set of animal movements.

3. Invite students to work in groups of three. Direct each group to choose three of the animal categories you discussed together and create a movement sequence.

4. Give students an opportunity to perform their sequences. Ask the class to analyze the types of movements they observed and then identify the animal categories.

Ideas for More Differentiation
Tap into students' verbal/linguistic capabilities by guiding them to write a haiku or other short poem about an animal. Invite student to improvise a dance or other movements illustrating the words of the poem.

Nature in Motion

Objective

Students will use dance to interpret movements found in nature while changing levels in space.

Students can explore levels of movement by interpreting some of the movements seen in nature. Moving at high, medium, and low levels in space creates interest and balance in dance.

1. Use a large, open space for this activity. Begin with students seated in a discussion circle. Ask them to think of different ways things in nature move. Ask students where these things move (e.g., *in the sky, on the ground, in water, in air*).

2. Ask students to name things that move up high (e.g., *fireflies, birds, clouds, wind, butterflies*) as well as low (e.g., *snakes, worms, tree roots, moles, beetles, grass, sharks*). Ask students if there are things that move somewhere in between high and low (e.g., *bees, drifting leaves, airborne seeds*).

3. Have students work in groups of three and choose a level—high, medium, or low. Allow them time to improvise movements that show something moving at that level. Invite the class to watch, guess the level, and guess the moving thing or animal being mimicked.

4. Have each group member choose a different level. Invite groups to decide to move together or one at a time at different levels. Encourage students to paint a scene with their movements. For example, they might be a cloud changing shape in the sky (high), tall grass blowing in the wind (medium), and a snake slithering (low). Another group might be the moon traveling in the night sky (high), a firefly dancing and twinkling (medium), and a child sitting on the ground watching (low).

Ideas for More Differentiation

Invite students to write a brief nature story in their journals. Have them include something moving at each level—high, medium, and low.

Looking Through a Window

Objective

Students will create a collage of a window view.

Materials

collage picture books

heavy drawing paper

collage materials (paper and wallpaper scraps, felt, gift wrap, tissue paper)

scissors, glue

black construction paper

Encourage students to see with an artist's eye! In this authentic task students use collage materials to represent what they see from a window.

1. Explain to students that collage is using pieces of different kinds of materials to make a work of art. Some artists break things into shapes, like a puzzle, and use various textures in their works. Show students some examples of collage from picture books. *I Love to Collage!* by Jennifer Linsey Edwards *You Can Make a Collage* by Eric Carle

2. Invite students to look through a window to observe what is outside. Explain that in this activity, they will make collages of something they see through the window.

3. Students can begin their collages with a pencil sketch on heavy drawing paper, or they can simply glue on different-shaped collage materials. Provide a variety of collage materials for students to glue onto their sketch to make the collages.

4. Give students four strips of black construction paper to glue around their collages as a window frame. Invite students to name their collages or verbally describe what their collages represent. Display students' artwork around the classroom.

Ideas for More Differentiation

Have students make a second collage by changing their window scene from day to night, from city to country, or to a different season.

Exploring Textures

Objective
Students will experiment with textures and create a textured work.

Strategies
Problem-based learning

Rehearsal

Materials
Tex T. Lion reproducible
textured materials (burlap, corrugated cardboard, corduroy, sandpaper, comb, lace, brick, wood)
drawing paper, crayons

Give students opportunities to explore various textures that lend dimension to their artwork. In this problem-based activity they can investigate and decide on which textures to use.

1. Provide textured surfaces and materials, such as burlap, sandpaper, cement, brick, lace, cardboard, combs, or anything with bumps or ridges. Have students place drawing paper over the surfaces and rub the paper with the side of a crayon.

2. After students have explored all the textures and discovered the different patterns and designs they make on paper, give them a copy of the **Tex T. Lion reproducible (page 88)**.

3. Have students select different textures for each part of the lion and color the entire drawing. Encourage them to think about what texture would be good for the lion's furry body, its fluffy mane, and its tail.

Ideas for More Differentiation
Invite students to reinforce their knowledge of texturing by creating textured self-portraits. They can make an outline drawing and use different textures to color hair, clothing, and skin.

Tex T. Lion
Directions: Choose different textures for each part of the lion. Place your paper over the textured surface, and rub it with the side of a crayon.

Tex T. Lion Page 88

Tex T. Lion

Directions: Choose different textures for each part of the lion. Place your paper over the textured surface, and rub it with the side of a crayon.

My Musical Memory

Objective
Students will respond to music by writing and illustrating a vivid musical memory.

Materials
My Musical Memory reproducible

Allow varied opportunities for students to respond to the arts creatively, physically, and emotionally. Music is a part of our lives almost every day. This authentic task invites students to share their own personal musical stories.

1. Tell the class about a childhood musical memory you have. You may recall a time when you heard a marching band in a parade, heard your uncle play in an orchestra, played the jingle bells in a school concert, or heard your big sister playing her favorite songs over and over.

2. Invite students to think about a musical memory they have. Maybe they received a guitar from a grandparent, heard their mom sing in a choir, woke up to hear the *Sesame Street* jingle, or danced to a band at their cousin's wedding.

3. Ask students to think about why that musical memory is special to them. Give students a copy of the **My Musical Memory reproducible (page 90)**. Invite students to write about and illustrate their musical memory. Encourage them to describe the event, explain how it made them feel, and why it is special to them.

4. Bind students' stories into a book for the class to share.

My Musical Memory Page 90

Ideas for More Differentiation
Invite students to write about musical instruments. Students who play a musical instrument can write about why they chose to play it, how to play it, and who inspired them to play. Others can write about an instrument they would like to play or their favorite instrument.

Name _____ Date _____

My Musical Memory

_____

_____

_____

_____

_____

_____

_____

_____

 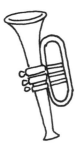

Reproducible

Read Me an Opera

Objective
Students will compose music to accompany a story.

Materials
familiar fairy tale
rhythm instruments

Strategies
Authentic task

Cooperative group learning

Multiple intelligences

Opera often tells stories of mythic proportions accompanied by music. Use a favorite children's fairy tale to give students experience with the authentic task of creating an opera. It's simple and fun to do, and it taps students' musical/rhythmic intelligence.

1. Select a favorite fairy tale, such as *Goldilocks and the Three Bears,* to read to the class. Ask students to listen for the different characters in the story. Ask: *What do they say? How would they sound if we could hear them?*

2. List the story characters: Goldilocks, Papa Bear, Mama Bear, and Baby Bear. Demonstrate various rhythm instruments, and ask students to listen and decide which ones could be used to represent different characters.

3. Divide students into groups so there is one group per story character. Ask each group to use rhythm instruments to create a short musical phrase for their character. Consider giving a maximum number of beats for the songs, such as four to eight counts, to limit their length.

4. Read the story aloud again, and pause after each character is mentioned or speaks. Invite each group to play their musical phrase each time their character appears in the story.

Ideas for More Differentiation
Challenge individual students or groups to compose a song (simple melody and words) to represent their character. Invite them to sing it while you read the story aloud.

Alphabet Rap

Objective
Students will compose and perform a rap.

Materials
Alphabet Rap reproducible
chart paper

Students love to create songs and raps! Invite them to develop rhythmic skills as well as reading and writing skills through this authentic composition activity.

1. Invite students to compose an alphabet rap. Provide a rhyming couplet as a model, such as: **A** is for **a**quarium, where fish like to **swim**. **B** is for a **b**luebird on a tree **limb**. Guide students to note the format of the couplet—each sentence includes a word that begins with the target letter, and the last word in each sentence rhymes with each other (*swim/limb*).

2. Divide the class into groups of three. Give each group a copy of the **Alphabet Rap reproducible (page 93)**. Assign each group an alphabet letter pair, and have group members write the two letters in the boxes on their reproducible.

3. Challenge each group to create a rhyming couplet following the sample format. Encourage them to use the rhyming word pairs if they need help.

4. After each group has written a couplet, organize groups in alphabetical order by the letters they were assigned. Invite groups to recite their rap at the appropriate time as you move through the alphabet.

Alphabet Rap Page 93

Ideas for More Differentiation
Invite students to work in small groups to compose a rap that teaches younger students about eating healthy snacks.

B is for a bluebird on a tree limb.

Alphabet Rap

Directions: Create a two-line alphabet rap. Be sure the last word in the first line rhymes with the last word in the second line. Use the rhyming word pairs for ideas.

> **Samples:**
> **A** is for **aquarium,** where fish like to **swim**.
> **B** is for a **bluebird** on a tree **limb**.
> **C** is for a **cat** that sits on the **fence**.
> **D** is for a **dime** that equals 10 **cents**.

☐ is for _____

☐ is for _____

Rhyming Word Pairs

above—glove	climb—time	funny—honey	slip—zip
ape—grape	corn—horn	kick—pick	song—strong
batter—platter	crash—flash	mouse—house	throw—glow
chair—pair	eyes—wise	pet—sweat	toes—nose
clear—ear	fence—cents	pour—floor	wide—cried

Mozart's Magic Flute

Strategies
Focus activity

Performance

Objective
Students will listen to a Mozart duet and make puppets move to the music.

Materials
Magic Flute Puppets reproducible
colorful craft items (feathers, glitter, buttons, fabric scraps)
glue
wide craft sticks
recording of "Papageno–Papagena" duet from Mozart's *The Magic Flute*

Give students some background about the great composer Wolfgang Amadeus Mozart. Mozart was a child prodigy. He began to play music at age three and learned to write musical notes before he knew the alphabet. Though he received serious musical training from an early age, he remained a fun-loving person in adulthood. This playfulness is especially evident in his opera *The Magic Flute.*

1. Play a recording of the "Papageno–Papagena" duet from Mozart's opera, *The Magic Flute.* Explain the story behind the music: *Papageno is a lonely bird catcher. He helps his friend Tamino on a magical journey. At the end of the opera, Papageno finds the bird woman of his dreams, Papagena! Together, they sing a happy duet in which they look forward to their marriage and children.*

Magic Flute Puppets Page 95

2. Give students a copy of the **Magic Flute Puppets reproducible (page 95).** Invite them to create Papageno and Papagena puppets from the figures. Direct students to color and cut them out. Provide colorful craft items for students to glue to their puppet costumes, and then have them glue their finished puppets to craft sticks.

3. Play the recording of Mozart's duet again, and invite students to listen carefully to determine who is singing. When they hear Papageno sing, invite them to make his puppet dance. When they hear Papagena sing, they can make her dance. If both are singing at once, both puppets can dance!

Ideas for More Differentiation
Have students work in small groups to choreograph their puppets' movements. Have them practice and give a performance for the class.

Magic Flute Puppets

Directions: Color and cut out the puppets. Glue craft items to their costumes. Glue each puppet to a stick. Then make your puppets dance to Mozart's music!

Papageno

Papagena

References

Agriculture in the Classroom. (2006, October). *Oats, peas, beans and barley grow.* Retrieved September 17, 2006, from www.agclassroom.org/teacher/pdf/prairie/prek_1/song.pdf.

Barata-Loren, M. (1995). *Mathematics their way.* Menlo Park, CA: Addison Wesley Publishing Co.

Barrett, P. (2001). *National Geographic dinosaurs.* Washington, D.C.: National Geographic Society.

Cullinan, E. (Ed.). (1992). *Invitation to read.* Newark, DE: International Reading Association (IRA).

Cunningham, M. (1995). *Phonics they use.* New York, NY: HarperCollins Publishers.

Edom, H. (1992). *Science with water.* London, England: Usborne Publishing Ltd.

Gregory, G., & Chapman, C. (2002). *Differentiated instructional strategies: One size doesn't fit all, second edition.* Thousand Oaks, CA: Corwin Press.

Hale, G. (Ed.). (1997). *Read-aloud poems for young people.* New York, NY: Black Dog & Leventhal Publishers.

National Council for the Social Studies. (2002). *Expectations of excellence: Curriculum standards for social studies.* Silver Spring, MD: National Council for the Social Studies (NCSS).

National Council of Teachers of English and International Reading Association. (1996). *Standards for the English language arts.* Urbana, IL: National Council of Teachers of English (NCTE).

National Council of Teachers of Mathematics. (2005). *Principles and standards for school mathematics.* Reston, VA: National Council of Teachers of Mathematics (NCTM).

National Research Council. (2005). *National science education standards.* Washington, DC: National Academy Press.

Zarnowski, M. & Gallagher, F. (1993). *Children's literature and social studies.* Washington, D.C.: National Council for the Social Studies (NCSS).